Contents

Acknowledgements
Text by Brian Stocks. Artwork by Bob
Currier. Photographs on back cover,
inside back cover, page 1 and page 4
courtesy of Supersport. Photographs
on front cover and inside front cover
courtesy of Allsport UK Ltd. The
publishers would like to thank
Continental Sports Limited for their
photographic contribution to this
book.

CONTINENTAL

Note Throughout the book gymnasts, teachers and coaches are referred to individually as 'he'. This should,
of course, be taken to mean 'he or she'
where appropriate.

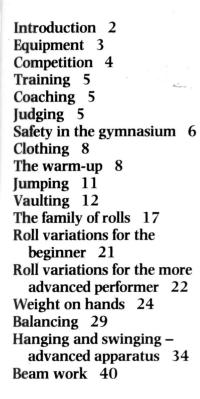

Introduction

During every Olympic Games, world audiences are amazed by the level of technical difficulty and athleticism achieved by the gymnast. Gymnastics is now ranked in the top group of spectator sports at the Olympic Games, having an even greater following than swimming. The Eastern European nations have dominated the sport at international level for many years, but recently this dominance has been threatened by the increasing success of the USA. As a direct result of the high profile achieved at these major events, gymnastics has become a popular participation sport, practised widely in clubs and in schools.

This book is offered to the coach, the teacher, the gymnast and the spectator as a means of gaining a practical understanding of gymnastics at its most basic level. It will also give an insight into the preparation and the skills that are essential if you are to develop as a competitor in the sport.

Gymnastics, like any sport involving dynamic movement and rotation, is one in which safety is vital; and safety precautions and good preparation must always be undertaken before engaging in and practising the sport.

It is essential that all coaches, teachers and gymnasts read thoroughly the section on safety (*see* pp. 6–7) before embarking on any gymnastic activity.

Internationally, gymnastics is under the control of the FIG (Fédération Internationale de Gymnastique). The sport is divided into five clearly defined disciplines.

- **Men's Artistic Gymnastics**, in which men and boys compete on Floor, Pommel Horse, Rings, Vault, Parallel Bars and High Bar.
- **Women's Artistic Gymnastics**, in which women compete on Vault, Asymmetric Bars, Beam and Floor.
- **Sports Acrobatics**, in which men's pairs, women's pairs, women's threes, mixed pairs and men's fours compete using their colleagues as the apparatus. This discipline also includes tumbling.
- **Rhythmic Gymnastics** (for women only) using hoop, ribbons, clubs, rope, ball and free exercise.
- **General Gymnastics** which covers the areas of Special Needs, Pre-School, Adult, Display, Festivals and Trampette Work.

For information on gymnastics in Great Britain, contact the British Amateur Gymnastics Association, Ford Hall, Lilleshall National Sports Centre, Nr. Newport, Shropshire TF10 9NB. For information on gymnastics outside Great Britain, contact the Fédération Internationale de Gymnastique, Rue des Oeuches 10, Case Postale 359, 2740 Moutier 1, Switzerland.

Equipment

The apparatus should be of the proper specifications and should be checked regularly to make sure that it has not become worn or damaged. Equipment used for competition is normally approved by the Fédération Internationale de Gymnastique.

Care must be taken in planning the layout of the gymnasium so that the gymnasts do not injure themselves when working on or dismounting from the equipment. Coaches and teachers should check the apparatus regularly to make sure that it has not been tampered with or moved. Where appropriate they should also alter the height of the adjustable apparatus so that it is suitable for junior performers.

Note Apparatus heights are normally fixed by competition organisers for the relevant age group, but if you have any doubts you should consult the nominated teacher or coach who has overall responsibility.

● School apparatus will vary greatly but will usually include the following fundamental pieces: individual mats; small hand equipment; small apparatus; large apparatus; fixed apparatus.
● Always place apparatus in such a way that landings and dismounts will not put the performer at any risk.
● Always check that the apparatus is not too close to doors, windows and radiators when designing your layout.
● Apparatus should be laid out with sufficient space between pieces.
● Never use apparatus that you do not feel confident working with.
● Apparatus must never be used without a responsible qualified adult or qualified coach in attendance.
● Always have your school gymnasium equipment checked and maintained at least once a year by a qualified company and keep a copy of

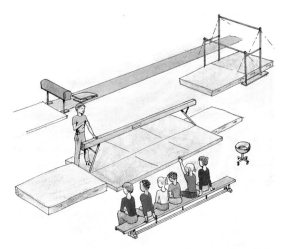

▲ *Fig. 1 Showing a well-spaced, safe gymnasium layout and good class discipline*

the written report. Your local authority or national governing body will be able to advise on recognised companies which are contracted to do this work.
● Never use a piece of equipment which is faulty or has been condemned, even if it looks sound and in working order.

Now read the section on 'Safety in the Gymnasium', pp. 6–7.

Competition

If you are in training for gymnastics you will be asked before long if you would like to take part in a competition. This involves building sequences (routines) on selected pieces of apparatus and performing them in front of a panel of judges.

Women

Women and girls compete on Vault (crossways), Asymmetric Bars (Uneven Parallel Bars), Beam and Floor. When you first start gymnastics you will normally just compete on Floor and Vault.

Men

Men and boys compete on Floor, Pommel Horse, Rings, Vault, Parallel Bars and High Bar.

Compulsory and Voluntary Routines

Competitions are divided into two main types: *Compulsory* and *Voluntary*.

The sequence of movements for Compulsory Routines is designed for you. Every gymnast must attempt to perform the same skills in the same way.

In Voluntary Routines you are free to include your own elements, and you choose to select difficult elements to raise your difficulty score. Of course, you must be able to perform them well so that the judges are not able to deduct too many marks for poor execution.

Normally the level of difficulty required as a minimum is laid down by the competition rules, and your routine should match that level of difficulty if you do not want to receive deductions for being short on content.

Training

Gymnasts need many qualities to be top-class performers, including discipline, strength, endurance, flexibility and spatial awareness.

Many gymnasts may be born with ability in one or several of the areas indicated, but to learn the whole range of skills involved in the sport requires considerable dedication and training. A top-class gymnast will train six to seven days a week for one or two sessions each day. Each training session can last several hours. Learning the basic skills can easily be achieved in one session a week, but as the skills become more difficult the amount of time spent training will have to be increased.

Coaching

All gymnastic activity should take place in the presence of a qualified coach or teacher. A coach is responsible for the safety and care of gymnasts under his control.

Judging

At gymnastics competitions the routines are normally marked by a panel of judges. The panel usually consists of four judges who sit around the apparatus, and a master judge who sits at the master judges' table.

Fig. 2 Judging a floor exercise ▶

The four judges mark the routines out of ten, deducting marks for errors or for routines which do not contain the required difficulty.

The four scores are passed to the head judge, who eliminates the highest and lowest mark and averages the remaining two.

Example

Judge	1	2	3	4
	9.60	9.80	9.50	9.70

The master judge ranks the four scores and removes the highest and lowest.

Judge	2	9.80
	4	9.70
	1	9.60
	3	9.50

He then averages the middle two scores.

Judge	4	9.70
	1	9.60
Total		19.30

Average (total divided by 2) = a final score of 9.65

While the four judges are writing down their score, the master judge also marks the routine. This is in case the four scores vary wildly or the difference between the middle two is too great. A sliding scale of differences is published by the International Federation FIG. The master judge's score is added to the gymnast's final score and the average is used as a base mark to try and resolve the differences. Sometimes a judge will change his score after a judges' meeting because of this base mark; at such a meeting the master judge will check the reasons for the variation in marks.

A panel of six judges is now being used to judge men's competitions at the Olympic Games and World Championships. Additional referees check the difficulty of the performed routines. Computers are used to perform the mathematics, and videos are taken so that judges can see the routines again if there is a dispute over the scoring.

If you would like to become a judge you must attend an official course run by your national governing body. To judge at international level you need to pass a Brevet course and hold a current Brevet card.

Safety in the gymnasium

Gymnastics is not a dangerous sport as long as it is properly planned and care is taken. Injuries normally occur through negligence or lack of planning. To ensure a completely safe gymnastic environment, four aspects need to be considered:

- layout of equipment;
- learning of new skills;
- performer safety;
- the teacher/coach.

Layout of equipment

- The first duty of the coach is to ensure that the apparatus is safe to use before work commences. It must be firmly anchored to the ground where appropriate, with all cables and fixings sufficiently tightened to minimise excessive movement.
- The apparatus should be well spaced so that there is sufficient room

for the gymnasts to mount and dismount, and in case the gymnast should fall. Always allow for the unexpected.

● If the apparatus is not mounted over a foam safety pit then sufficient mats must be arranged beneath and around it. Ensure that there are no gaps between the mats. Use large safety mattresses (30 cm or 8–12 in thick) to make the area even safer.

● All apparatus should be correctly erected, secure and upright with guy ropes properly anchored.

● The gymnasium hall should be clean; floor surfaces should not be slippery, especially if children are encouraged to work in bare feet.

● Ensure that the gymnastic apparatus is stored safely and neatly. It is better to store apparatus around the hall than in one area, as children can access it more easily if necessary.

Learning of new skills

● Gymnastic training should only take place in the presence of a qualified gymnastic coach or teacher. The coach or teacher must be in attendance at all times.

● A performer must warm up thoroughly before starting more strenuous training, and difficult skills should be introduced slowly or possibly broken into key component parts to remove high levels of anxiety.

● When in the process of learning a new movement, or performing any movement which involves a degree of risk, a gymnast should always be in the presence of a coach.

● If the coach is concerned about the safety of the performer then additional matting should be placed around the apparatus in case the gymnast should fall. In situations involving inversion a safety mattress approximately 12 in (30 cm) thick should always be used.

● The learning should be sufficiently progressive so as not to tax the gymnast too far.

● Gymnasts should never be allowed to work beyond their level of ability.

● The coach should be capable of giving assistance to the gymnasts if necessary and supporting them if they get into trouble.

In gymnastics, many performers will be young children; therefore the responsibility for safety will fall heavily on the coach/teacher. This will be important when considering the size of the group and the level of control the coach/teacher can offer to the performer. It may be necessary to progress at a slower rate with a larger group. **The gymnasts' safety should be ensured at all times.**

Performer safety

● The performer should be properly dressed.

● The performer should be thoroughly warmed up.

● The performer should be trained and conditioned in parts of the new skill before attempting the whole element.

Clothing

Competition clothing

Men's costume has changed little over the years. The International Federation Code of Points states that on Pommel Horse, Rings, Parallel Bars and Horizontal Bar all competitors must perform their exercise in long, solid-coloured competition pants and footwear (gymnastics slippers or socks). On Floor and Vault the gymnast may wear short pants and perform without footwear. The wearing of a competition jersey is mandatory in all competitions.

Women's competition clothing has certainly changed a lot since the first British team appeared way back in the 1928 Olympics in gym slips, long knickers and thick socks. Now gymnasts wear brightly coloured, long-sleeved leotards for competitions. The gymnast must wear a leotard with wide shoulder straps – narrow shoulder straps are not allowed. The leg cut of the leotard may not extend beyond the hip bone. Gymnastics slippers and socks are optional.

Training clothing

● Children should be suitably dressed for work on apparatus and should not wear socks without suitable shoes.
● Loose baggy clothes which may catch on the apparatus should be removed or tucked in.
● Long hair should be tied back.
● Jewellery that might be unsafe to the wearer or to others should be removed. Rings and earrings should always be removed.

The teacher must be aware of the need for his or her own clothing, footwear, jewellery and hair to conform to safety standards.

The warm-up

> It is essential that performers are thoroughly warmed up and prepared before undertaking any gymnastic activity.

Please read the section on safety before undertaking any practice.

Correct warm-up and body preparation are essential elements in any training programme. The gymnast and coach must quickly get into the habit of warming up at the beginning of every practice session, however short, and on no account must the warm-up be omitted.

Warm-up should prepare the body and lay the foundations for the strenuous work that is to follow. You will also find that it will have a positive mental effect so that gymnasts will often feel better and more ready for work as a result of it.

Value of the warm-up

- Prepares the body for exercise;
- helps to prevent injury;
- helps to improve motivation.

The warm-up generally consists of running and jogging activities designed to raise the overall body temperature, closely followed by stretching and limbering exercises and basic body conditioning. It must be carefully taught to young gymnasts to stop them attempting skills without their body having been properly prepared. Whilst warming up, participants should wear plenty of clothing, including a tracksuit and sweatsuit if available.

The warm-up should consist of activities which will prepare the cardiovascular system. It should stretch and prepare the muscles, associated ligaments and connective tissues for the forthcoming work, and contain work that will relate to the main activity which is to follow. Finally, it should prepare the neuromuscular system and contain mobility exercises to prepare the joints.

For the warm-up to be fully effective, it must prepare all the body systems:

- *cardiovascular, cardiorespiratory* – heart, lungs, blood vessels;
- *muscular-skeletal* – bones, muscles, tendons, ligaments, connective tissue;
- *neuromuscular* – circulation, body, brain.

Typical warm-up

A typical warm-up begins with general jogging, running and skipping around the gymnasium until the body feels as if it is warm. Exercises which use the majority of the gymnast's muscles should be included, such as arm and leg swinging and trunk circling. Games such as tag chain, leap frog and catch are also good motivators in the case of young gymnasts.

Once the body begins to feel warm the gymnasts should progress to more specific suppling exercises, mobilising and exercising all the major joints – for example wrists, elbows, shoulders, neck, back, hips, knees and ankles. When these joints have been sufficiently manipulated then, under the instructions of a teacher/coach, the performer can look at increasing the range of movement of these joints while adopting a range of suppling activities (*see* 'Flexibility', page 10).

◀ *Fig. 3 A warm-up, incorporating running, dance and jogging activities, stretching and limbering, and basic body conditioning*

9

Flexibility or suppling

This is a method whereby the range of movement of a particular joint or muscle group is increased.

A good level of flexibility is essential, not only because it allows for the correct body position to be developed but also because maximum range of movement will minimise injury when muscles are accidentally over-stretched.

Many basic movements will be difficult for children and gymnasts who have not achieved sufficient suppleness within the joints. It is surprising to note that despite our modern lifestyles a large number of children are unable to place their hands fully above their heads or even to sit on the floor with their backs at 90° to the ground.

As a guideline, the minimum warm-up duration should be 5–10 minutes for a lesson of 25–30 minutes. Ideally the activities chosen will relate to the work which will follow and to the skills which are to make up the main part of the lesson – warm-up activities can help with the learning process.

▲ *Fig. 4 A range of suppling exercises designed to mobilise and exercise the major joints fully and safely*

Jumping

Standing upward jump

- Bending your legs slightly, jump quickly.
- At the same time raise your arms upwards and forwards to a position above your head. Keep your arms in front of your body.
- As you land your feet should be slightly apart at an angle of 45° ('Plié') and your knees flexed.
- Try to land still with your arms raised over your head.

Coaching / teaching note If the performer throws his arms too vigorously upwards there will be a tendency for his shoulders to move backwards.

Astride jump from box

- As you leave the box top, spread your legs and arms as much as possible so that your body forms a star shape in the air.
- On approaching the floor, quickly bring your legs together and attempt to land still without any extra movement of the feet.

Standing upward jump with full turn

- Perform the upward jump as described opposite.
- To initiate the full turn you must push strongly with your feet in the direction of the turn, and raise your arms more forcefully across your body to assist the spin.
- It is important to keep the body fully stretched throughout this movement, as this will allow the full turn to proceed more easily.
- Try to 'spot' a place before taking off for the jump. If you look for that place as you land it will assist the landing phase. This technique is known as *spotting*.
- Once again, by bringing the arms down to the side and keeping them stretched out you will slow the spin down to help with the landing.

Coaching / teaching note Make sure that the gymnasts try this on soft mats, so that they can land safely should they lose their balance. Young children find this skill particularly difficult due to their relatively large heads.

▲ *Fig. 5 Astride jump from box*

▲ *Fig. 6 Standing upward jump with full turn*

11

Tucked jump from box

- Bend your legs and swing your arms down to your knees.
- Quickly straighten your legs and at the same time swing your arms upwards and forwards.
- At the height of the jump, quickly bend your legs and bring your knees up to your chest, then just as quickly stretch out again in preparation for the landing.

▲ *Fig. 7 Tucked jump from box*

Coaching / teaching note The coach should stand to one side of the gymnast and take hold of his chest to make sure the performer does not over-rotate.

12

Vaulting

The Vault is one of the first pieces of apparatus that should be introduced to the beginner gymnast. Vaulting is an exciting and exhilarating activity, suitable for all ages as long as the height of the Vault has been suitably adjusted.

The vault is divided into seven distinct phases:

- approach run;
- hurdle step;
- take-off;
- pre-flight;
- strike;
- post-flight;
- landing.

▲ *Fig. 8 'The vault is divided into seven distinct phases...'*

Every vault requires these phases to come together in harmony. A good vault consists of an aggressive approach followed by a very powerful dynamic flight and strike movement. The gymnast is attempting to transfer as much power as possible from the run-up to the components of height and rotation.

The gymnast and coach should spend the initial learning period mastering the approach run and take-off from the springboard. It is important to have a consistent run-up and to be able to take off from the springiest part of the board every time.

There are two types of vault:

● *horizontal*, in which the heels rise on take-off and return to the floor after the strike phase;
● *vertical*, in which the heels continue to rise after the strike phase and pass over the head to the floor.

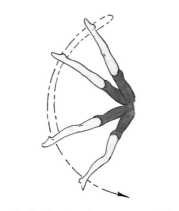

▲ *Fig. 9 Showing the movement of the heels in a horizontal vault*

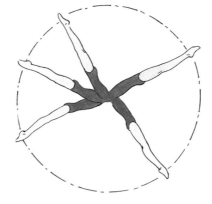

Fig. 10 Showing the movement of the heels in a vertical vault ▶

Squat on to and jump off box with straight body

● From a short run and hurdle step (in which the feet are hopped together) land with two feet in front of the box.
● Place your hands on to the box top and, jumping hard from the floor, raise your hips and simultaneously squat your feet close to your hands.
● In order to raise the hips sufficiently it is important to press strongly against the box top. Allow the shoulders to move forwards slightly over the hands as the hips are raised.
● Jumping off the box, quickly straighten your legs and stretch your body, placing your arms over your head.
● Keeping your head up in the jump, quickly focus your attention to the spot on the floor where you are going to land.
● On landing, bending at the ankles, knees and hips absorbs the energy from the jump.

Coaching / teaching note It may be necessary to assist the very young gymnasts in one of the phases. In the first phase support can be given from the side, by taking hold of the gymnast under his near shoulder and stomach. In the jump-off phase, the coach should stand either to one side or in front of the gymnast and take hold of his chest, controlling the rotation of the performer so he achieves a safe and steady landing.

Straddle vault over buck or cross-box

● From a short approach, run and hurdle step.
● Jump upwards and forwards, quickly placing your hands on the box top. Push strongly.
● As the hips rise, straddle your legs and allow your shoulders to move slightly forwards over your hands.

● As you strike the box top your body will begin to rise.
● Once in flight, bring your feet together whilst at the same time quickly stretching your body.
● Concentrate on keeping your chest up and preparing for the landing.

Coaching / teaching note A strong push will carry the gymnast over the box and return his feet to the ground. Beginners have a tendency not to push strongly enough.

▲ *Fig. 11 Squat on to and jump off box with straight body*

14

Practice

Beginners can be encouraged to straddle on to the box top with support. The coach should stand in front of the gymnast, supporting his chest close to the arms. At the appropriate moment he can help him over the box after several practices. The supporter should be aware of the possibility of the gymnast catching his feet on the box – a common fault since beginners tend not to straddle their legs sufficiently. Due to this possibility you are advised either to support the performer or to place the appropriate soft safety mat on the other side of the Vault where he will land.

◄ *Fig. 12 Straddle vault over buck*

Headspring

The box will be a cross-box. This can be lowered to assist the first part of the movement, especially if the gymnasts are very young.

● Approach this vault with a short run and a hurdle step on to the springboard.
● Place your hands centrally on the box and jump, raising your hips well above your shoulders.
● As the hips rise, and are at about hip height, bend your arms and place your head lightly on the box top.
● Your body will be bent at the hips.
● As the hips pass over the hands and head, push strongly with your arms, at the same time extending the hips and driving your heels upwards and forwards in the direction of flight.
● Arch your body and continue to push against the box top until your arms are fully extended.
● Maintain this extended body position until your feet contact the floor.
● On landing, bend your legs. Keep your head up.

▲ *Fig. 13 Headspring vault*

Coaching / teaching note The coach should be aware that the higher the vaulting box, the more difficult the first flight and the easier the second flight. The lower the box, the easier the first flight and more difficult the second flight. He should vary the height of the box to suit the size and ability of the children in the group. Place suitable matting in the landing area as the gymnast can land with an arched back in the early stages of learning this skill.

As a useful training aid the coach could make the approach side of the box lower by placing two benches side by side for the gymnasts to work off. This would allow a slightly higher box to be used.

Handspring

This vertical vault has sometimes been referred to as a *longarm vault*, but the modern term for it is now handspring. It is one of the hardest skills by far to perform correctly, as the body has to be raised some considerable height above the ground with sufficient rotation to be able to regain the standing position.

- To obtain the necessary height and rotation a fast but controlled approach run is required.
- On take-off you must drive your arms upwards and extend the body.
- You must think of the lower body rotating over the upper body.
- You must still be moving upwards at the point when your hands strike the Vault.

- The angle of the body with the Vault should be between 60° and 80° to the vertical in the strike phase.
- Your hands should leave the horse just before your body reaches the vertical. To achieve this the strike phase must be short and extremely powerful.
- During post-flight keep the body as straight as posisble.
- Bend the body slightly prior to landing and flex the knees.

Coaching / teaching note This movement will require tremendous coordination of speed and power. The beginner will find it particularly difficult to raise his body to the required position without losing rotation and power. The coach should be prepared for a poor second flight and should stand on the landing side of the Vault, supporting the upper back to assist the rotation back to the feet. If the performer is unable to complete a strong strike phase his wrist should be grasped with the coach's second hand as he strikes the box. This will prevent him from over-rotating. If the coach reaches over the box he will be able to give a little lift to any gymnast needing more rotation.

▲ *Fig. 14 Handspring vault*

The family of rolls

Rolling is the most basic and fundamental skill in gymnastics. It is important that great care is taken to master the technique correctly, as many of the basic shapes and controls that are used in the more complex skills are developed at this early stage.

Basic position for the family of rolls

● Lying flat on your back, draw your knees up to your chest. Curl up tight making a rounded back, then rock backwards and forwards, holding your knees tightly.
● Rock backwards and forwards with a little more power. When your feet make contact with the ground, stretch forwards with your arms and attempt to stand.
● From standing, crouch down, roll back on to your shoulders and rock back to your feet.

Forward roll (see page 18, fig. 15) ▶

Forward roll

● From standing, crouch down. Place your hands on the floor in front of you, shoulder-width apart with your fingers facing forwards. Bend your legs while simultaneously placing your chin on your chest. This action will ensure that your hips are raised high enough and your spine is rounded so that you can roll on to your back.
● The arms are then bent as you place your neck on the floor. It is the bending of the arms that causes the gymnast to overbalance into the rolling action. He can continue to roll on to his feet.
● Try to keep your legs straight as you commence the roll forwards. In the very last part of the roll bend your legs tightly so that your heels are close to your bottom.
● At the point where your feet make contact with the floor, stretch forwards with your arms so that your head and chest move over your feet. Once your body-weight is in a position of balance you will be able to stand.

Coaching / teaching note Beginners will find it a temptation to use their hands to help them stand. This should be avoided at all costs.

A spotter can help in the final phase of this movement by standing in front of the gymnasts and taking hold of their arms to help them to get to their feet.

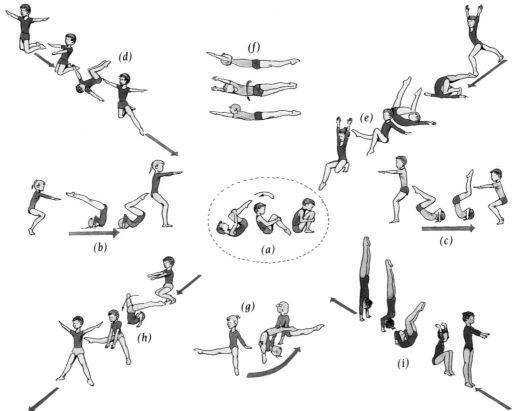

▲ *Fig. 15 The family of rolls. Showing from (a) to (i): the basic position; forward roll; backward roll; tucked sideways roll; sideways roll; log roll; tin soldier roll; forward roll with straight legs to straddle (Method 1); backward roll through handstand*

18

Backward roll

● From standing, lower to a squat position with your back well rounded.
● Allow your body to move backwards so that your body-weight falls back over your heels until your bottom makes contact with the floor.
● The body then rolls backwards to the position where the shoulders make contact with the ground. As this happens move your hands quickly to a position just above your shoulders, with your fingers facing and your palms away from your body, elbows held high.
● As the rolling movement takes place put your chin on your chest so that as little weight as possible is put on your head.
● When your shoulders make contact with the floor, push against it strongly with your hands by straightening your arms. This raises the hips slightly and takes the weight off the head.
● The body continues to rotate, still maintaining the curled position, until the feet make contact with the ground. The movement is finished in a squat or standing position.

Coaching / teaching note The backward roll may be supported by a teacher, who takes hold of the gymnast's waist at the point at which he rolls on to his shoulders. The supporter can then gently lift the gymnast's hips over his head to aid the actual rolling movement, whilst at the same time reducing the amount of weight felt by the gymnast on his head.

As the head of most junior gymnasts is larger than the rest of the body, many of them will find this movement quite difficult. They will tend to twist and turn the head and roll over one shoulder. This is an acceptable way of rolling, but they should be taught very quickly how to roll while using their hands to support their body-weight so that the turning of the head does not become a habit which would be difficult to break at a later stage.

Tucked sideways roll

● From a tightly curled position, hands and knees drawn closely to your body, allow yourself to fall to the side. Ensure that you maintain the curled position.
● Roll over your back and return to the hands-and-knees starting position.

Coaching / teaching note The teacher can stand over the performer, assisting and guiding him in the correct alignment of the roll and for the final phase back on to his feet.

Sideways roll

● Start with one leg stretched and one knee bent (*see* below).
● Lower your body forwards while simultaneously tipping sideways. Roll on to your back. Bend the outstretched leg to allow the body to roll *across* the back.
● At the point at which the alternate knee makes contact with the floor, stretch the opposite leg to arrive back in a mirror image position of the one in which you started.

Long sideways roll (log roll)

● Lying flat on the floor, lift your feet and hands slightly whilst keeping them stretched. Move both your hands and your legs to one side.
● As the weight is transferred and your body tips on to its side you will begin to roll. Draw your arms and legs back into a straight-line position with the rest of the body, arms above your head, feet stretched below your body.
● As your body continues to roll, bring your arms back behind your head while hollowing and extending your legs backwards.

● You will now roll on to your stomach.
● By continuing to stretch your arms and legs in the direction of the roll, you will now roll from your stomach on to your side.
● At this point you can bring your arms and feet forwards slightly, allowing yourself to roll on to your back.

Coaching / teaching note Most beginners will be able to do this roll with their arms and legs on the floor, so even the less able child will be able to complete rolling using this technique.

Tin Soldier roll (circle roll)

- Sit on the floor, legs in straddle.
- Take hold of your legs just below the knees.
- With a slight dynamic movement of the body to the left or the right, topple over on to your shoulder.
- By folding more tightly towards the legs you can roll across the middle of your back and return to the original sitting position.
- As this movement requires no change in position once the overbalancing has been achieved, the performer is able to retain a fairly rigid body shape without moving in order to complete the roll.

Coaching/teaching note The teacher/coach may need to stand behind the performer to help him roll on the correct part of the shoulders – from the middle of the back to the shoulder blades. The common problem is that beginners do not roll high enough across the shoulders and therefore find this movement quite difficult.

Roll variations for the beginner or very young child

Rolling with a platform

Many performers have difficulty in standing up at the finish of a forward roll. Sitting on the end of a platform, rock backwards and forwards and then stand.

▲ *Fig. 16 Rolling with a platform*

Rolling from a box top

Using two or three sections of a box and an additional landing mat, lie on the box on your stomach. Move forwards so that your hands and chest are overhanging the box and can be placed on the mat on the ground. By slowly adjusting the amount of weight which is resting on the box top and transferring it to your hands you will be able to lower your body on to your upper shoulders. Then, by curling your body, commence the roll.

▲ *Fig. 17 Rolling from a box top*

Roll variations for the more advanced performer

Forward roll with straight legs to straddle

● While rolling over your back in a forward roll your legs must be kept straight. As you approach the lower part of your back in the roll, straddle your legs wide. The wider the straddle, the easier the movement is to perform.

Method 1

As soon as your heels touch the floor, place your hands on the floor (between your legs and close to the crutch). Push hard with your hands and lean well forwards. Try hard to get your head and chest in front of your feet.

Continue to press against the floor for as long as possible until your fingers leave the floor. Continue to bend your body forwards until your body-weight is completely over your feet; you will then be able to stretch out in the straddle stand position and raise your body.

Method 2 (slightly harder)

By following this method you can stand without using your hands on the floor.

As you make contact with the floor, press down on to the ground with your heels. Reach forwards with your arms and chest so that your bottom rises from the ground to a position of balance in line with your feet. The balance position is controlled and the forward movement of the body stopped by moving the arms backwards into the position of balance.

Fig. 18 Forward roll with straight legs to ▶
straddle (Method 2)

22

Backward roll to astride

The movement is started in the same way as the backward roll.

● As you roll over on to your back, and then on to your shoulders and neck, begin to straighten your legs.
● As soon as your hands are placed firmly on the floor, push strongly against the floor to raise your hips over your head.
● With the hips well raised, straighten your legs and place your feet on the ground in the straddle position (close to your hands).
● When your hips are directly over your hands, straddle your legs and lower your feet to the floor close to your hands to finish in a stride stand.
● To ensure you will actually finish in a stride stand it will be necessary to push vigorously with both hands. Your head and chest can then be raised to a position of balance.

Fig. 19 Backward roll to astride ▶

Coaching / teaching note A spotter or teacher can help the performer in the final phase of movement by supporting the hips when they reach their highest point. This will remove some of the weight from the performer's hands and assist him as he rolls over his head.

Backward roll passing through handstand

This is a natural extension of the backward roll to straddle/stand.

● Perform the first part of the roll in exactly the same way as for the backward roll to straddle.
● With this skill it is important to move the hands to the shoulders as quickly as possible.
● As soon as your hands contact the floor, ensure that they are in a position just above the shoulders, with the fingers facing the body and the palms away from the body. The elbows should be held high.
● When the hands contact the floor push strongly with both hands and arms, at the same time extending the hips and legs (straighten the body) towards the ceiling.
● Hold your head in by placing your chin on your chest.
● Timing is the key to this movement, as the extension to the ceiling and the arm push should happen simultaneously and at such a rate that the body is extended towards the vertical.

This movement can be learnt progressively by practising the basic backward roll, while concentrating on pushing the hips to the ceiling and simultaneously stretching out the legs.

Coaching / teaching note The coach/teacher/spotter can help the gymnast by taking hold of his feet as his hands contact the floor. They can then lift him through the movement, drawing his feet to a position above his hands into a straight handstand. For this movement to be performed correctly the body should momentarily pass through a held handstand position.

Weight on hands

Bridge

● Start from lying on your back.
● Draw your knees up so that your feet are close to your bottom.
● Stretch your arms above your head, bending them so that your elbows are raised towards the ceiling and your hands are placed on the floor with your fingers pointing back to your shoulders.
● Your hands should be close to your head. (Be careful not to trap any long hair.)
● From this position push against the floor with hands and feet so that your bottom and back are raised from the floor to arrive in the bridge.

▼ *Fig. 20 Bridge*

● The movement is complete when both arms and legs are completely straight. Make sure that your ankles and knees are pressed tightly together.
● The ideal bridge position, depending on the suppleness of the performer's shoulders, is one in which the shoulders lie directly over or in fact slightly in front of the hands.

Coaching / teaching note It will be necessary at first to assist the beginner, as this position is not easy to attain until the required flexibility in the shoulders and spine have been developed, along with sufficient strength to support the full weight of the performer. Support can be given by lifting the gymnast under his shoulders as he tries to adopt the bridge position. At the very beginning it is easy for the gymnast to hold the supporter's ankles.

● **A bridge is a four-point balance.**

Cartwheel

The key to success in this movement is the ability to be able to do both a handstand and a side handstand with legs straddled. Although it does not stop the beginner practising a simple cartwheel, the coach must be aware that it is particularly difficult if the gymnast is unable to master these two prerequisite skills.

At the start of this movement you can either face the direction in which you intend to go or stand sideways. The method described here is the former.

- Raise your hands above your head and place your leading leg forwards.
- At the start your arms should remain overhead as the leading leg is placed forwards on to the floor.
- Reach forwards to place the first hand (the hand on the same side as the leading leg) on the floor by bending your front leg and also bending at the waist.
- When the first hand makes contact with the floor, straighten your front leg while at the same time kicking it upwards with your back leg over your head.

- Continue the movement by rocking over from your first to your second hand (which is still extended above your head). To do this, push strongly against the floor with your first hand, keeping your arms stretched up over your head.
- As your body rocks over your second hand, your second leg is brought down to the ground and placed close to your second hand.
- Starting with your left leg, the sequence of movement is left foot, left hand, right hand, right foot.
- The whole sequence should be completed in a straight line.

Coaching / teaching note Emphasise the point of pushing strongly with the second hand so as to arrive in a stretched standing position. To assist the gymnast in performing this movement a coach/teacher can stand to his rear. If the gymnast leads with his left leg the spotter should place his right hand on the gymnast's left hip, i.e. with his hands crossed, left arm over right arm. The supporter is then able to help the gymnast to move through the side handstand as well as aid the overall rotation and the final phase of arriving back on the feet.

▼ *Fig. 21 Single cartwheel with support*

25

Preparation 1

Standing on all fours straddling a line, jump from one leg to the other over the line.

Preparation 2

Stand one side of a line. Place one hand on one side of the line. Simultaneously jumping your legs over the supporting hand, place the second hand over the line and allow the feet to drop to the ground.

Preparation 3

A circle is drawn on the ground. The performer stands on the circle and places his first foot, his first hand, his second hand and his second foot on the points around the circle while his eyes look at centre of the circle.

Coaching / teaching note The performer should be encouraged to get his hips and shoulders directly over his hands.

▲ *Fig. 22 Cartwheel preparation 1*   ▲ *Fig. 23 Cartwheel preparation 2*

▲ *Fig. 24 Cartwheel preparation 3*

Two cartwheels

In this skill two cartwheels are performed, one after the other, exactly as described above. However, the second cartwheel will always be done from a sideways-facing position.

As described earlier, it is important on the first cartwheel to push hard with the second hand as it makes contact with the floor. This will increase the speed of the movement for the second cartwheel and allow it to proceed smoothly from the first.

Bend your legs slightly as your feet come into contact with the floor. Your feet should be turned out to facilitate the necessary control coming into the first landing and the push going into the second cartwheel.

Coaching / teaching note   If the legs are kept perfectly straight there will be a tendency to hesitate before moving into the second cartwheel. The performer should concentrate hard on moving down a straight line.

When this skill is performed correctly the gymnast will have no problems in doing a series of cartwheels in continuous fashion. When performing a series it does look very much like a coach wheel rolling down a mat.

▼ *Fig. 25 Two cartwheels*

Round-off (Arabian spring)

This movement is developed directly from the cartwheel and is basically a cartwheel with a quarter-turn during the hand placement phase. In a cartwheel, both hands and feet move along a straight line; but in a round-off the second hand is placed slightly out of alignment with the first.

The round-off is a key movement in gymnastics, turning forward movement very efficiently into backward movement. There are several variations on the basic skill, but in all cases a good strong push from the hands is required.

● The round-off turn is made on the first hand. As the speed of the movement increases, the hands must be placed further apart. It should be noted that as both hands contact the floor the legs still trail behind the body in the direction of travel.
● Starting with a small run and a skip-step, stretch the arms overhead. If you are leading with the left, the skip-step consists of the following ground

contact: right foot, right foot, left foot, hand placement.

● Lean well forwards. Bend the leading leg, and also bend at the waist to place your left hand on the floor.

● Immediately and quickly straighten your left leg, while at the same time swinging your right leg upwards into a cartwheel action.

● Your body will simultaneously twist around the left hand so as to place the right hand out of alignment with the left.

● As soon as both hands are in contact with the floor the legs, which are trailing behind in the direction of travel, are snapped down to the ground. Push hard with your hands at the same time. (This is all happening while the quarter-turn is completed.)

● In a good round-off you should land facing the direction from which you have come, with your feet either side of an imaginary line. In this way the forward movement is transferred into backward movement.

● Land with your arms raised above your head, and your body in a semi-crouched position (see fig. 26) with your back well rounded.

● In a round-off which is done to stand, the feet are placed away from the hands. In a round-off which continues into another movement, such as a backward roll or a backflip, the feet are placed closer to the hands.

Coaching / teaching note The round-off is best done in stages. First the gymnast should perform a cartwheel with a quarter-turn, bringing the second leg to meet the first. He then repeats the movement several times, each time reducing the time the second leg takes to join the first. Eventually he will bring both feet together in flight simultaneously so that he lands with his feet together. Finally the round-off is performed from a couple of running steps with the emphasis on bouncing out of the landing. The correct shape for the round-off is essential and the performer should endeavour to arrive in the position shown in fig. 26.

Preparation 1

Performing a round-off from a springboard will help the gymnast push out of the skill and encourage the necessary flight from the hands.

▲ *Fig. 26 Round-off or Arabian spring*

Fig. 27 Arabian spring preparation 1 ▶

28

Preparation 2

Performing the round-off over a mat will encourage the performer to obtain the essential flight and strong push from the hands.

▲ *Fig. 28 Arabian spring preparation 2*

Balancing

Arabesque

This movement relies heavily on the flexibility or range of movement of the performer. The coach should be actively encouraging improvement in flexibility, working on it during the warm-up.

● Start by standing on one leg with the other leg stretched behind you, the top of your big toe resting on the floor.
● Raise the free leg upwards behind you, keeping your back straight.
● Fix your gaze on some point in front of you; this will help you to maintain your balance and to receive visual feedback of any movement occurring in your body.
● Continue to raise your leg to the full extent of your suppleness.
● As you raise your leg, continue to lower your chest. Keep your head up; this will allow your back to hollow.
● You can choose whether to lift your arms forwards or to the side. The aim of

the coach should be to make sure that the arms follow the hollow line made by the raised leg; he should help the gymnast to position the arms so that an aesthetic pose is achieved. The necessary angles in the shoulder will be obvious to the coach, but may not be possible for the performer to achieve if he does not have the required suppleness.

▲ *Fig. 29 Showing the arabesque with different arm positions*

Bridge

The bridge as described on page 24 is also a movement that can be performed under a 'balancing' theme.

29

Headstand from crouch position

● Crouch down and place your hands and forehead on the floor to form a triagle (*see* fig. 30(b)) Your head should be approximately 30 cm in front of your hands and your arms bent at an angle of 90°. The pattern drawn by your head and hands should be an equilateral triangle.

● By pressing with your hands, slowly move your bottom over your forehead into a balanced position. Maintain the equilibrium by continually pressing with your hands.

● By exerting more pressure you will reach a point at which you can lift your feet from the floor.

● Continue to raise your legs above your head by pressing constantly against the floor with your hands. Make sure that your back is kept straight at all times by tightening the muscles of your bottom and stomach.

● As your legs move above your shoulders you will need to draw your bottom back slightly to prevent yourself from toppling over.

● To maintain balance it should feel as though your body is 'wishing' to return to the ground, and that this is only being prevented by the constant pressure exerted through the hands.

▲ *Fig. 30(a) Headstand from crouch position*

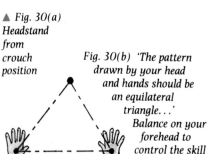

Fig. 30(b) 'The pattern drawn by your head and hands should be an equilateral triangle...'
Balance on your forehead to control the skill

Coaching / teaching note A spotter can help the gymnast by taking hold of his hips and making sure that he adopts the correct position while assisting him to find his balance.

Headstand with knees bent

● Start from crouch.

● Place your hands and forehead on the floor to form a triangle (*see* fig. 30(b)) with your head approximately 30 cm in front of your hands.

● Your arms should be bent at 90°, elbows pointing to the ceiling.

● Slowly move your feet in closer to your hands until your hips lie above the triangle base.

● Push down strongly with your hands on the floor. Your feet will leave the floor and you will feel for the balance position.

● Your knees should be bent tightly with your back held straight. This straight-backed position allows your weight to be evenly distributed over your hands and head.

Coaching / teaching note The gymnast should be encouraged to maintain a straight-backed position. There will be a tendency for him to hollow his back, thus placing excessive pressure on his head and neck.

Handstand with support

The handstand is one of the key basic positions in gymnastics and it is well worth spending time to learn it. It is required in the development of many other skills. Initially the handstand should not be attempted without support; the role of the supporter is described in the coaching/teaching note opposite.

▼ *Fig. 31 Handstand with support*

- Start from a standing position with your arms raised over your head, shoulder-width apart.
- Take a long step forwards, bending the front leg. Place both hands on the floor approximately shoulder-width apart, fingers facing forwards.
- Straighten the front leg while at the same time kicking and thrusting the back leg into a position above your shoulders.
- As the driving leg nears the position of balance, bring your other leg to join it so that both legs arrive simultaneously in the handstand position.

Coaching / teaching note It is important that the shoulders first move forwards over the hands, returning to a position directly above the hands once the handstand position has been achieved. This creates the feeling of balance and is something that the gymnast must learn.

Constant pressure is maintained through the fingers to maintain balance. The handstand itself must be absolutely straight: if a straight line was drawn from the point of contact with the floor – i.e. the hands – to the feet, it should pass straight through the middle of the body.

The supporter must stand facing the gymnast, who places his hands on the ground just in front of one of his partner's feet. The supporter then grabs the gymnast by the hips, assisting his arrival in the balance position. Once in the balance position, the supporter should only 'feather support' the gymnast so that he is able to control the skill himself.

The supporter can also check for the straight position which is so essential to a successful handstand.

Remember that the gymnast must do most of the work and therefore must not be over-supported. The coach should be careful to make sure that the gymnast is in a vertical position, thus learning to balance on his hands.

Handstand

A natural progression from the handstand with support (*see* page 31) is the handstand held freely.

● The gymnast should ensure that his body is held quite straight, with the emphasis upon complete extension of the shoulders and a straight-line relationship between arms, body and legs.

● The gymnast should be encouraged to point his toes towards the ceiling.

● It is very important to avoid letting the body-weight simply rest on the hands; concentrate on pressing the body up as far as possible.

Coaching / teaching note There must be constant pressure between the heel of the hand and the fingertips. For equilibrium to be achieved the balance point must remain between the heel of the hand and the tips of the fingers. Because the relative strength of the arms is far less when supporting the body in handstand, the balance position is very critical and will take some time for the beginner to learn.

Practice

One way to learn this movement is to balance against a wall. Note that before attempting this the gymnast must be able to support his body-weight on straight arms, and demonstrate this to a supporter.

● Place your hands approximately 20–30 cm from the wall and kick to handstand (*see* page 31).

You must be able to kick to handstand and return to the floor – by pressing against the wall with the heels – without collapsing.

● Once you have mastered this confidently, move your hands closer and closer to the wall until your fingers are about 12.5 cm away. You will then be

Fig. 32
Practise your handstand against a wall ▶

forced into achieving a straight handstand, because if the body is bent in any way you will be forced back down to the ground.

● Once you are successfully able to kick to a handstand with your fingers almost touching the wall, you must learn to tense the muscles in your body – and especially in your bottom – so that it is under constant tension and as straight and as stiff as possible.

● Then, by applying constant force through the fingertips, you will find that your heels will drift slightly from the wall. By constantly applying and releasing this pressure you will be able to remain in this position with your feet very close to the wall but not actually touching it. It is particularly important that you 'feel' the overbalance position.

Coaching / teaching note The more flexible a performer, the less the force that is required actually to hold the handstand position and therefore the less force that has to be caught and balanced on the hands. It is very important that the coach work on suppleness so that the gymnast can achieve the correct position with the minimum of force.

Eventually the coach should encourage the gymnast to start practising the handstand in the middle of the gym floor, learning to kick into a held position. The movement will have been thoroughly learnt when the gymnast can arrive in handstand without bending his arms or 'walking' his hands to regain balance.

Special note

When the gymnast first attempts this on the floor there is a strong possibility that he will overbalance. He needs to be taught how to turn out of the movement, and sufficient matting must be placed on the ground so that he can roll out of the movement if necessary.

The next skill is to kick to handstand and hold the balance perfectly still for 3 seconds or more. A lot of practice is required if the gymnast is to deliver the right amount of force to arrive in the handstand, and to continue to apply the pressure through the fingers to prevent himself from overbalancing.

Fig. 33 Handstand on a bench – good ▶
preparation for the Beam

Balance 'versus' equilibrium

The use of the word *balance* in this situation is probably incorrect. More accurately, the gymnast aims to achieve a state of *equilibrium* in which the heel of the hand is the balance point for the body, and which is maintained by way of a constant force applied through the fingers. Many beginner gymnasts throw themselves into a position on their hands without understanding the role played by their fingers and the forces in their arms in maintaining the handstand. The coach must emphasise the importance of this role.

Handstand on bench

Once the handstand has been mastered on the floor it can be attempted on a bench. This is a good preparation for transferring the skill to the Beam.

● Place your hands on the outside edges of the bench, with your thumbs facing fowards and your fingers gripping the under-edge of the bench. This will give you good leverage.
● Then adopt the same method of kicking to handstand as described on page 31. If you perform the movement with confidence you will find that gripping the bench helps you to create the necessary force and to control your balance much more efficiently.

Coaching / teaching note   The coach should be aware that the gymnast is likely to topple over, and teach him how to turn out of the skill by moving one of his hands forwards and cartwheeling down on to the floor. Additional matting should be placed where he may fall. This is not a suitable movement for the gymnast who is not competent in rescuing an overbalance situation, as the height of the bench makes it quite difficult to roll.

Hanging and swinging – advanced apparatus

Cast/beat to handstand on low bar

● Starting from support on the bar with hands in overgrasp or undergrasp, bend forwards.
● Move the bar position from thigh to waist.
● Swing your legs forwards at the same time as you bend forwards, then drive your legs forcefully/quickly backwards simulanteously pressing down on the bar with your hands.
● Keep the shoulders low whilst the legs swing to an inverted position above the bar.
● The body will need to be tense when it is straight in order to transfer the swing from the legs to the rest of the body.
● This straightening of the body will cause the body to rise upwards towards the handstand position and the arms can be locked straight.

Practice on the floor

The gymnast should practise handstand push-ups on the floor to improve shoulder strength. He should be discouraged from hollowing his back.

▼ *Fig. 34 Cast to handstand on low bar*

Safety note It is extremely important that once the beginner gymnast starts achieving handstand he is able to dismount either way from the bar – i.e. he can fall forwards or backwards from handstand. It is essential that he learn this particular skill on a low bar, so that he is aware of the various options available to him.

Coaching / teaching note Most gymnasts will *not* be able to achieve this forceful extension of the legs and hips with sufficient power and energy to arrive in the handstand position. The beat to handstand requires a delicate combination of swing and strength.

Upstart

The upstart movement on low bar, Parallel Bars and Rings is very similar, but a slightly different technique is required in each case.

Upstart on low bar

The upstart basically allows the gymnast to move from a position of hang to a position of support – i.e. from a position below the bar to a position above the bar.

- The gymnast stands facing the apparatus with the bar at shoulder height.

- Jumping upwards off the ground and simultaneously reaching forwards to grasp the bar the gymnast pikes slightly at the waist, allowing the body to swing with the hands in overgrasp and the legs stretched out in front (the *float*).
- When the body is as far forwards as possible it is extended into a straight line with the shoulders pressing back against the bar.
- As the return swing begins, the performer bends rapidly at the waist, bringing his feet in close to the bar.
- As the body swings back under the bar the gymnast drives back forcefully with the legs to the straight line position at the same time pressing down with his hands and arms on to the bar.
- The bar is then pushed along the body – without making contact with the legs – from the ankle to the thigh. This action is completed as the body continues to rotate up into front support.

Coaching/teaching note The hands must be moved around the bar in advance of the body's rotation to allow for a strong front support position to be achieved. A common fault with all beginners is that they rotate around the wrist and not around the bar, thus arriving on top of the apparatus with their hands forced backwards into a position which prevents them from supporting themselves properly on the apparatus. It is important to note that in the case of most skills it is normal for the fingers to be trailing around the bar, but in the upstart the body works against the fingers thus requiring the hands to be shifted very quickly to the required position.

◀ *Fig. 35 Upstart on low bar*

Parallel Bars

Nearly all work done on the Parallel Bars is part of the 'swing' family of gymnastics. Exercises on Parallel Bars must consist of *swing*, *flight* and *held* elements, and may also contain a certain amount of strength work. Swing and flight must always predominate, however.

Due to the nature of the apparatus, special attention must be given to the development of swing and support strength. Coaches and teachers should also note that apparatus which is designed for adults may not be suitable for young gymnasts, and buy special adaptation kits in order to reduce the distance between the bars. The bars should be roughly shoulder-width apart: a good indication is to place the elbow and hand between them. If the performer is able to touch with elbow and finger-tips then the bars are at a suitable width.

Swinging on Parallel Bars

- The swing is a pendulum movement in which your shoulders move forwards and your feet backwards.
- Your shoulders move backwards as your feet swing forwards. This is to keep your balance on top of the bars.
- Swing from the chest and shoulders with a slight kick of your feet at the bottom on the forward swing.
- Hold the body straight.

Upstart on Parallel Bars

- Swing forwards in hang maintaining complete extension in the shoulders. Your feet will glide forwards just above the bars due to a slight flexing at the hips.
- As you reach this fully extended position, quickly bend at the hips and bring your feet to your hands.
- Swing back in this position, bringing your legs close to your face.
- As your shoulders begin to rise on the return swing, extend your hips forcefully and perform a strong downward push through straight arms to raise the body to front support.
- The upward thrust is therefore created during this latter part of the swing, which is a backward and upward pendulum movement.

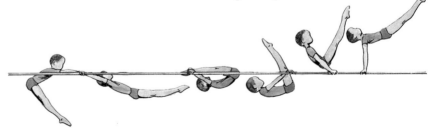

Fig. 36 Upstart on Parallel Bars ▶

Swing to handstand on Parallel Bars

This skill should first be approached by practising using two chalk lines drawn on the floor to indicate the bars. The lines should be shoulder-width apart.

Having successfully mastered kicking to handstand on the two lines without moving the hands, the gymnast can transfer to two benches, starting with the benches side by side.

● Kick to handstand from the benches.
● Slowly widen the gap between the two benches until it is equivalent to the width of the performer's shoulders.

To transfer this skill to the low Parallel Bars, start on the end of the bars facing outwards. Kick to handstand and then finally attempt the swing to handstand.

● If you fail to make handstand you must move the shoulders forwards to come down in the swing in control. Failure to do this will result in a risk of the arms collapsing.

● If you kick or swing too hard you can turn out of the movement into a quarter-turn, or drop over on to the safety mat which has been placed at the end of the bars.
● Once you have mastered the skill successfully on the end of the bars you will be able to transfer it to the middle. Extra care must then be taken if you topple over, as you must push strongly from one arm to come down on one side of the bars.

Coaching/teaching note The coach should support this skill in the first instance by holding the gymnast's shoulder with one hand whilst lifting his hips with the other.

Swinging on the Rings

The Rings offer a unique challenge to the gymnast because of their instability.

● Keeping your hips and shoulders tight, initiate the swing from your shoulders. Keep your arms straight.
● At the end of each swing, push the rings away from you and slightly apart.
● Maintain pressure on the rings at all times.
● Your body should rise upwards in the swing due to its pendulum motion and to the downward pressure of the hands.

◄ *Fig. 37 Swing to handstand on Parallel Bars*

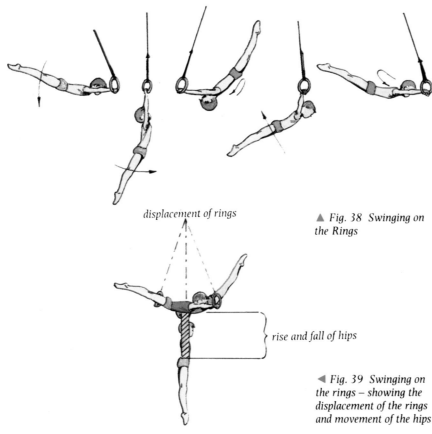

displacement of rings

▲ Fig. 38 Swinging on
the Rings

rise and fall of hips

◀ Fig. 39 Swinging on
the rings – showing the
displacement of the rings
and movement of the hips

Upstart on the Rings

The upstart is one of the basic methods
of getting above the rings and of
moving from hanging to a position of
support.

● Start from inverted hang with your
feet above your head and your hands at
the side of your body.
● Pike deeply with your knees drop-
ping very close to your face without
pause. Then extend your feet forcefully
to the ceiling in an upward and forward direction whilst simultaneously
pressing down on the rings towards
your hips. This will bring your shoulders up above the rings.

Coaching/teaching note The rings must be
kept close to the body to maintain control.
Once the legs have been forcefully extended
away, the key to this skill is to flex quickly at
the hips and maintain a piked position
during the upward and forward movement
of the body. This movement is created
through alternate flexing and contracting
of the legs and trunk.

Handstand on Rings

The handstand is more difficult to perform on Rings than on Floor or Parallel Bars because of the unsteady nature of the apparatus.

● The handstand should be held without the arms or body touching the wires. Control should emanate through the wrist and not through the shoulder.

● To achieve the correct position the rings should be turned slightly outwards, with the gymnast's thumbs turned away from one another. This will help bring the arms into a straight position.

Coaching/teaching note The handstand is best practised on 'lower' rings – i.e. kicking up from a low box or pressing up into the position from a raised platform. Two spotters should be used to stabilise the rings by pulling down on them on both sides while the gymnast learns to balance on them. It is important that the gymnast is able to control the handstand successfully on Floor before attempting this skill on either Parallel Bars or Rings.

▲ *Fig. 40 Upstart on the Rings*

▼ *Fig. 41 Handstand on the Rings*

Beam work

In principle, the exercises performed on Beam are technically the same as those performed on Floor, with slight variations induced by the narrowness of the apparatus. Many of the exercises practised on Floor can be transferred with the minimum amount of difficulty, but care must be taken as the Beam is only 10 cm wide and with every movement is the possibility of falling.

To gain confidence you should start by practising the skills on a low bench, then transferring them to a low beam, etc. Some of the more difficult moves should be practised with a mat over the Beam.

One of the most important aspects of Beam work is posture, and from the very beginning composure and control are essential. General practice should include the following.

● Walking briskly along the Beam keeping hips and shoulders in line.
● Jumps, jetés, split jumps.

● Turns. All turns and pivots should be performed on the toes. As you turn, raise your arms above your head and rise up on to your toes.
● Turns on two feet. Standing with one foot in front of the other, extend your legs and ankles until you are on your toes. At the same time swing your arms up and slightly to one side, creating a twist at the shoulders. Push through the front leg and perform a half-turn, taking the weight evenly on both feet.

▼ *Fig. 42 Squat-on mount on to the Beam*

Squat-on mount

● Face the Beam.
● Place your hands on the Beam, shoulder-width apart.
● Jump from both feet and press down with the hands.
● As your hips rise, squat your feet between your hands.
● Transfer your weight to your feet and stand up.

Coaching/teaching note Beginners have a tendency to lose their balance as their feet squat to the Beam. Support them under their shoulder so they have good control.

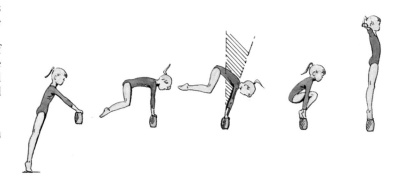

Straddle mount from front support

- Place your hands on the Beam with your fingers just over and gripping the far edge.
- Jump to front support.
- Push on one hand and swing the leg of the same side over the Beam. Simultaneously transfer your weight to the other hand.
- As your leg rises above the height of the Beam, and begins to swing forwards over the Beam, momentarily raise your free hand to allow it to pass over the apparatus.
- On replacing the hand, quarter-turn the body to face the supporting hand and sit astride the Beam.
- Place both hands in front of you and press down, allowing your shoulders to move forwards. As your legs swing backwards, bring them up to squat on to the Beam.

Half-spin on one foot

- Step forwards on to an extended leg and foot.
- Raise your arms above your head to initiate the turn.

- Hold your head up. When you have completed the turn fix your gaze back on the end of the Beam.
- You can turn inwards or outwards. The inward turn is normally easier.

▼ *Fig. 44 Half-spin on one foot*

Fig. 43 Straddle mount from front support ▶

Forward roll on Beam

Initially this skill should be practised on a bench. Note that the hands will have to be closer together to grip the beam and to support the weight of the body at the start of the roll.

● Your thumbs should be along the Beam, your hands down the side.
● The roll should be performed fairly quickly but with good control.
● Finish the roll as you would on Floor, but place one foot slightly in front of the other.
● Reach well forwards with your arms, and when your weight is on your feet stand up.

Coaching/teaching note Placing a mat on the Beam and taking hold of the performer's hand or arm as she attempts to stand up will greatly assist her in this movement.

Cartwheel on Beam

Practise this on a line on the gymnasium floor, and have your coach check that each hand and foot makes contact with the line.

● The cartwheel is the same as a cartwheel performed on Floor except for the fact that the head and eyes now watch the Beam all the way through the movement.
● The second foot is placed closer to and facing the hands. For better grip the foot can be placed slightly at an angle across the Beam so the toes can grip the edge of the apparatus.

Coaching/teaching note The performer may have difficulty placing her feet back on to the Beam after the support on hands. The coach positions himself so that he can support the gymnast in this second phase. If the Beam is too high the coach should stand on a box top or platform.

Handstand on Beam

This movement should be performed initially on the floor or on a floor beam.

The gymnast can adopt the same process as when performing the handstand on bench, or perform the movement with a quarter-turn in handstand. The method described here is for the handstand with the thumbs running down the Beam.

● The handstand can be performed with the legs straight, split, or with one leg bent and one leg straight (this is called the *stag* position).
● The technique is exactly the same as when performed on Floor except the thumbs are placed along the Beam and the fingers down the side of the Beam.
● The back leg is kept straight. The arms are raised above the head in the early stages.

Coaching/teaching note The coach should assist the performer until she has gained confidence and is fully aware of what to do if she kicks too hard.

Advanced gymnastic skills

Splits (forwards or sideways)

In learning the splits, stand with your legs wide apart and place both hands on the floor. Gradually move your feet out wider until tension can be felt in the adductor muscles (those muscles on the upper part of the inside leg). Hold this position for 10–20 seconds and then relax. Repeat two or three times. In time you will reach the full splits position.

Forward splits

● The knee of your front leg should be facing upwards and the knee of your back leg facing downwards. Your toes should be pointed.
● Your body should be facing directly forwards.
● Your arms should be raised above shoulder-level but the final position is optional.

Side splits

● The knees in side splits should generally be facing upwards. However, depending on the position of the body, the hips and the knees can be facing forwards.
● The body must be held upright with the back flat. There must be no arching of the back.
● In both types of splits arms should be held horizontal or higher.

Coaching/teaching note Improving flexibility should be a careful and gradual process, especially in the case of young children. It is not recommended that the coach try and improve flexibility by applying pressure, as this requires a high degree of skill and damage can easily be done to young bones and muscles.

Practice

Sit facing the wall-bars with your legs straddled as wide as possible. Grasp the bars at about chest height and try to pull your hips closer in to them while allowing your legs to slide out. At the point of maximum stretch, hold the position for a count of six then relax and pull the bars closer again. Finally hold the position for about 1 minute.

▲   *Fig. 46   A variation on the side splits*

◄   *Fig. 45   Forward splits*

43

Sequence work

Handstand, forward roll

- Kick to handstand and hold straight for at least 3 seconds.
- Stretch out in your shoulders and allow your feet to move forwards over your hands.
- Once you have overbalanced and you can feel the sensation of falling forwards, look for the spot on the floor where your shoulders will make contact.
- At the last moment duck your head under, placing your chin on your chest so as to allow the neck and shoulders to make the first contact with the floor.
- As your shoulders touch the floor, round your back and proceed into the forward roll.

Coaching/teaching note In the fall forwards from handstand there will be a tendency to bend the arms. This is quite acceptable, but as the gymnast becomes more competent he should be encouraged to try to keep the arms straight.

There will be a tendency for the beginner to collapse on the fall from the roll and to land heavily on his back. This is because his feet are moving backwards and his back is not sufficiently rounded.

Backward walkover

- Start from a stretched standing position with your arms above your head.
- Raise one leg forwards, extended and with the toe pointed, to a position between 90° and 180° to the floor. The height of the leg will depend on your level of flexibility.
- Your weight should be fully on the other leg.
- Extend your shoulders by pressing your arms fully back behind your ears and head.
- As you continue to press the arms backwards, allow your back to bend slowly and progressively from the shoulders down to your lower back until your hands are lowered on to the floor. Simultaneously thrust your hips forwards to counter the weight of the body bending backwards.
- Make sure that the hips remain square and do not twist.
- At the same time as your back is beginning to bend, lift your front leg over your head through splits position down to the floor.

◀ *Fig. 47 Handstand, forward roll*

- As your foot contacts the floor, push strongly with your hands so that the weight is transferred from the hands to the foot.
- Keep your back straight and pass through arabesque position to stand.
- Keep your arms stretched above your head by your ears throughout the movement.

Coaching/teaching note The coach can assist the performer throughout this movement. Standing at his side, he can support the middle of the gymnast's back with one hand whilst lifting the raised leg with the other.

Handspring

The handspring starts with a three-pace run-up and a skip step. The gymnast should be leaning slightly forwards in the upward phase of the skip step.

A long step into the handspring will assist the placement of the hands on to the ground.

- Bend your leading leg and place your hands on the floor in front of you.
- As your hands make contact with the floor, extend the leading leg while at the same time swinging the back leg upwards very fast towards the handstand position. The leg movements must be very fast and powerful.
- When your body-weight is completely on your hands, push hard from hands and shoulders, attempting to 'shrug' your shoulders to obtain even more lift. You must push from the floor with straight arms, to prevent your shoulders from travelling forwards over your hands.
- In flight your body should be slightly arched with your hands held over your head.
- You should attempt to land in an extended position whilst keeping your arms above your head by your ears.
- On landing, your knees should be slightly bent but your body should remain quite straight.

Coaching/teaching note The handspring is best learned from a raised platform with a safety mat. The coach should support the gymnast under the near shoulder and lower back, and in the early stages of learning should carry him through the entire movement.

▲ *Fig. 48 Backward walkover*

Backflip

This movement is one of the fundamental gymnastic skills and is essential to all advanced acrobatic and tumbling skills. It is therefore important that the gymnast develop a powerful and technically correct backflip for future improvement.

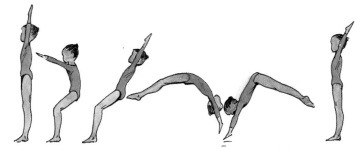

▲ *Fig. 49 Backflip*

● From standing, sit back into an off-balance position while swinging your arms downwards to a position by the knees. Do not lean forwards over your feet as you sit back.

● At the lowest point of the sit, reverse the action and begin to extend your body in a backward and upward direction. The body should be *unfolded* (rather than extended so forcefully that you jump).

● Press back hard on your heels and aim to keep your feet on the floor for as long as possible.

● During this extension phase your arms should be swung forwards, upwards and backwards.

● Allow your head to move backwards as your arms pass your head.

● Your body should now be arched with your shoulders completely extended.

● Your hands should make contact with the floor with your legs still behind them. You should think of your hands touching the floor before your feet leave it – in practice there will be a short flight phase.

● From this arched position, push strongly against the floor whilst at the same time snapping your feet to the floor by forcing the body into a piked position. These two actions of snap and thrust must happen simultaneously.

● Try to bounce out of the flip once your feet touch the floor again, as this will be good preparation for linking the backflip to other movements.

Coaching/teaching note Support is very important in the early stages of learning this movement and soft mats should be used where possible. The supporter stands to the side of the gymnast and holds him under his near thigh and lower back. Support should be given throughout the movement until the gymnast makes contact with his hands on the floor. If necessary the support should then be transferred to the snap-down phase to help the gymnast regain his feet. Many gymnasts jump too high in the take-off phase and this results in bent arms in the support phase. They should be encouraged to 'unfold' and to place their hands on the mat instead of jumping backwards on to their hands.

Advanced Floor agilities

Forward somersault

Fig. 50 *Forward somersault, showing the more common arm technique* ▼

[th]is movement starts with a three-
[pa]ce run-up into a hurdle step from
[on]e foot to land on two.

[A]s the feet make contact with the
[floo]r the body is allowed to rotate
[mo]mentarily around them, whilst
[sim]ultaneously jumping from the floor.
[Th]is forward and upward phase is
[kn]own as the *take-off*.

On take-off you should be leaning
[sl]ightly backwards as your feet make
[c]ontact with the floor. It is important
[th]at you do *not* lean forwards.

You should aim to keep the body
[u]pright during take-off.

You must obtain the maximum pos-
[si]ble amount of height without losing
[an]y rotational speed.

The arms are raised either forwards
[an]d upwards (common technique), or
[ba]ckwards and upwards (Japanese
[tec]hnique) at the instant of take-off,
[an]d this action must be almost com-
[ple]ted whilst the feet are still in contact
[wit]h the floor.

● It is the combined leg thrust and
arm action which will give you good
height and good rotation.
● Once in flight you should tuck the
body tightly to aid the rotation.
● When using the backward arm lift
(Japanese technique) you will grab
your legs behind your thighs; in the
forward arm lift you will grasp your
legs just below the knee.
● Just before landing, 'open out' by
quickly extending your legs. Keep them
slightly bent, however, so that you do
not land on a straight leg.

● In the early stages of learning this
movement keep your legs slightly apart
so that you can spot the landing more
easily. This will also prevent you from
hitting your face should you land
heavily.

Coaching/teaching note The coach should
assist the gymnast by taking hold of his
stomach at take-off. The gymnast then
rotates around the coach's arm. In this way
the coach can both support the gymnast
throughout the movement and help him
sense when to open out for the landing.

Body preparation and conditioning

The preparation of the body is the singular most important aspect in developing into a good gymnast. Many of the simple movements will be impossible without the right level of specific fitness. This is especially important in young gymnasts, as a good level of general conditioning is essential for the later learning of more advanced skills and techniques.

Good technique must be taught from the outset, but this is only possible if sufficient attention is paid to the relevant conditioning exercises.

The well-prepared gymnast scores highly in terms of *strength* and *endurance*.

● *Strength* is the amount of force that can be exerted at a moment in time by one maximal muscle contraction.
● *Endurance* is the body's ability to be able to perform a continual action over a period of time.

Index